Will our children b

WE ALL RESPOND
TO GRIEF IN
UNIQUE
WAYS...

IF WE
DIDN'T
WE REALLY
WOULD BE
UNIQUE!

HELPING YOUR CHILD THROUGH BEREAVEMENT

Mary Paula Walsh

VERITAS

First published 2000 by
Veritas Publications
7/8 Lower Abbey Street
Dublin 1

ISBN 1 85390 530 5

Design: Bill Bolger
Cover illustration: Angela Hampton Family Life Picturres
© Angela Hampton
Cartoons: John Byrne
Printed in the Republic of Ireland by Betaprint Ltd, Dublin

CONTENTS

INTRODUCTION   1

1   HOW WILL THEY REACT?   4

2   UNDERSTANDING DEATH   13

3   THE STAGES OF GRIEF OR HOW THEY MIGHT FEEL   17

4   CAN I/SHOULD I PREPARE THEM?   24

5   CHILDREN'S WAYS OF COPING   26

6   PROFESSIONAL HELP   30

7   CONCLUSION   32

To all those who helped me
with my childhood losses,
both then and now.

INTRODUCTION

Death is always shocking. Whether it happens suddenly or after a long illness, there is something immediately stunning about that moment from which there is no turning back.

Each death is of course quite different, as is each individual who dies and the circumstances of death. Each family reacts differently and in their own characteristic way. Children experience and react to death in this context and take their cue from those around them. As they get older, their peers and other outside influences also affect how they will react and grieve afterwards.

Contrary to what many adults think, children experience loss much like we adults do, though of course differently in some ways, which I will deal with later. So it follows that children need to grieve similarly to us in some ways and differently in others.

In helping bereaved children, the single most important thing to remember is that each child is a unique individual and will behave as that – uniquely and individually.

The most helpful thing you can do to help them is to *acknowledge* their pain. Let them know that you understand they are feeling bad. Often they cannot express or even realise why they are sad, angry, guilty, etc. They just know they feel awful and that *something* is terribly wrong.

Children in a big world, full of bigger, older people, a world that is now suddenly perhaps frightening and insecure, can and often do feel isolated and abandoned.

Their world and how they experience it and what happens to them is largely determined by their parents. Depending on their age, they have as yet few other experiences to compare this disaster with, and they have not yet developed a world-view to measure it by.

They need your time and attention. If you are just not in a place to give it, maybe you could find another sympathetic adult known to your children – an uncle, aunt, big sister or brother or grandparent, even a good friend or neighbour who could be a special friend to them at this difficult time.

Children often show their pain by what we call 'acting out' or behaving in a way that is difficult for adults to take at the best of times. When this happens we may think they are deliberately acting up, 'attention seeking' or using the situation as an excuse to get their own way. It is quite natural for you to feel exasperated, especially when you are feeling bad and/or guilty yourself. However, try to remember how *they* are feeling, but also that *you* have not got an unlimited supply of attention. Make sure you have someone to listen to *you*.

LOOK AFTER YOURSELF

Sometimes it is even harder to watch those we love, especially our children, suffer than to experience our own pain. If you have bereaved children it is likely that you are bereaved yourself. In these circumstances children can be both a worry and a life-saver. You worry and wonder if they will survive this terrible experience. Will they be okay or damaged permanently? Children can also be a practical distraction from your grief since they have to be looked after and/or given attention. Their resilience and energy can help you to find meaning again.

When you watch your children stunned and bewildered by a death, often feeling abandoned, guilty and fearful or any of the other powerful emotions engendered by death, it can seem almost more than you can bear. You need to do your own grieving. Perhaps you may need the help of loving and close family members or friends, or sometimes a counsellor or psychotherapist to do this. If you are grieving well and dealing and coping with all that death entails, your children will almost certainly come through the experience – changed irrevocably of course – but not scarred or damaged.

The first step in helping your children cope with a bereavement is, as they say on the aeroplane, tend to yourself first!

Remember, however, that grieving is a *process*, and once *you* have begun to attend to it yourself, you can *start* thinking about your children – don't wait until you have *finished* grieving or completed the process!

CHAPTER 1: HOW WILL THEY REACT?

How a child reacts to the death of someone close depends on many factors:

- Who has died – their relationship to the deceased
- The circumstances of death
- The child's make-up and personality
- The child's early life experiences
- The child's age and level of ability to comprehend
- How those around the child react
- The child's involvement with the dying, death, funeral and other rituals

WHO HAS DIED?

Death can be very frightening, even to the most mature of us. It can feel like the ground has shifted beneath us. So it is for children, only much more so, since their very survival often depends on their carers. So when the *primary carer*, or 'mother figure' dies, children will feel their survival threatened; the younger the child the greater the threat. As they get older this applies also to the 'father figure', or partner of the primary carer.

How the *death of a sibling* will affect children depends on how important the deceased was in their lives and how close the relationship. The same applies to grandparents and other close relatives and friends. If the death of a sibling results in your child becoming an only child and having to grieve without other siblings to share it with, he or she is likely to find grieving harder and will feel more isolated.

A *miscarriage* will affect small children largely through *your* reactions and the reactions of others around them. Older children may have been aware of the impending arrival and feel the loss more strongly.

Stillbirth and death of an infant are similar, but nowadays, when children may be brought to see the remains (depending on the circumstances), the death is brought home much more vividly and they will react more like they would to that of an older sibling, although perhaps not a very close one. This also depends on age and expectations.

DEATH OF PETS

The death of a beloved pet is very often the first encounter children will have with death. Do not underestimate their grief. The way that they, and you, handle this death can act not only as a first introduction to the subject, but as a model for all future deaths, and it can determine their attitude to death and their way of grieving.

A pet is often a child's best friend and its loss should be taken seriously as such, though the child will probably recover quickly.

If you can, have a funeral for your pet and *allow the child to plan it* and take charge of it. You could have a little 'wake' and invite other children, grandparents, etc. Let the child be involved in the burial. Most importantly, allow children to grieve and *never* ridicule them for grieving for an animal.

THE CIRCUMSTANCES OF THE DEATH
Sudden death is much more difficult for children to come to terms with. To very small and all pre-verbal children most deaths are sudden. It is likely to undermine their feeling of safety and stability in the world and make them anxious and fearful about what might happen to others close to them and to themselves. It can also give them an underlying feeling of uncertainty about life in general. Older teenagers are probably beginning to realise this about life in any case, but it can still be very traumatic. In earlier years it may affect them very deeply.

The sense of unexpectedness in a sudden death is actually of greater significance to children than the actual circumstances of death, though these can sometimes be very important. Sudden death in a road, car or plane accident, for example, could make them very fearful of travel.

When a death has been sudden, or appears sudden to children who have not been prepared, their stability is undermined and often they perceive their very survival to be threatened. They need as much reassurance as you can give them that their survival is *not* threatened, that *some* things will remain constant and especially that other adults on whom they depend, and any others they are close to, are not going to disappear suddenly.

The normal stage of disbelief and denial can be more difficult to move through with a sudden death. Therefore, anything that helps to bring home the *reality* of the death is important, especially seeing the dead person and being as involved as possible in the death, funeral and other rituals.

Suicide and murder pose the great dilemma – to tell or not to tell children. I believe this almost totally depends on their age and ability to comprehend. Certainly they should be told the truth at some stage, but for very small children perhaps later rather than sooner. There is no easy answer to the dilemma except to look inside yourself and trust your own instincts about your own children. You know best what is going to help them and what their strengths and levels of comprehension are. If you yourself are just too upset and involved with your own grief (quite understandably), consult someone close to you and the child, or possibly ask a professional counsellor.

Death after an illness will bring questions about ageing and illness. Take plenty of time to explain this to the best of your ability. Be open to discussion. Remind your children of people who have recovered from illnesses. Remember, they usually fear the death of a remaining parent when one has died. Reassure them that you are well and healthy (if you are). Explain the difference

For a while I was scared that everyone who got sick was bound to die...

So was I — but a little bit of explanation cured me.

between illness and life-threatening or terminal illness, and that the norm is for people to die when they are very old.

MAKE-UP AND PERSONALITY

As parents, you will be well aware of the individuality of each child and how, in the same family, children can be so different. They seem each to arrive with a set of gifts and their own particular problems, their individual strengths and weaknesses. It is with these that they will face and cope with their loss.

EARLY LIFE AND EXPERIENCE

The bonding and nurturing that a child receives from birth and the way weaning and early separation are handled all stand to help a child to cope with loss later on. The more secure the child feels as a result, the less they will be thrown by a shock such as death.

Early experiences of loss and separation, not only in early days from their mother, but also the loss of pets, the transition from home to play-school and first trips away from home and parents, all prepare the ground for more traumatic losses such as the death of a parent, grandparent or sibling.

Age

A lot of what is written regarding age and understanding is generalisation, but it can provide useful guidelines. Before the age of four, children have little concept of death, but that does not mean they cannot grieve and mourn the loss of someone close. Even tiny babies show anxiety when the parent/primary carer is missing for any long period. Most of their distress will come from the difference in their surroundings, and this includes their carers, after a death has occurred in the family. Older toddlers can understand loss and absence, i.e., that something/someone has 'gone', but they cannot grasp its permanence and often believe the deceased will come back the next day, week or whenever. They do not understand 'never' or 'forever' and just have to live through the endlessness.

At this age children often show their distress physically, for example by illness, refusing to eat, bed-wetting and tantrums. Reassurance is what is important and at this age it is mainly shown in a physical and practical way. Keep as many aspects of their world as constant as possible – the people and the environment they are used to, even the same food, cups, toys and other playthings. Hold and hug them plenty. Let them know where you are going and don't leave them alone for long periods if possible. If absence is unavoidable, leave them with familiar people. And *let them cry*, act out and be angry, even with you; who else can they be angry with?

By the age of five, children are usually beginning to grasp the concepts of permanence, irreversibility, cause and effect and the difference between being alive and being dead. They can be helped to arrive at this level of understanding by patient listening, answering questions and discussing the whole thing. Besides this, exposure to death in a non-frightening atmosphere is important. For example, they can come to understand the difference between being alive and dead by seeing people and pets who have died, touching and watching them and being allowed to ask questions. 'Protecting' them by keeping them away can be well-meant but is misguided and can even prolong the stage of denial.

Children up to the age of ten or eleven cannot sustain emotional sadness for long periods and usually manifest their grief through disturbed behaviour such as school phobia, stealing, bullying and difficulties in learning and relating socially.

Coming up to adolescence, and during adolescence, children begin to see and develop a view of death similar to adults, and also to grieve in some of the same ways. They become increasingly able to show their grief emotionally rather than through bodily symptoms and distressed behaviour (though they, and we as adults, often show our grief in these ways too).

At a time when young adults are striving to become independent, they find it difficult to cope with the feelings of helplessness and dependence that are a natural part of the grieving process. A parent's death can still trigger a lot of insecurity for teenagers, which they may interpret as 'childish'. Talk with your teenagers as much as possible. Take them into your confidence – without depending on *them*. Involve them in some decisions so they can still feel that they are regarded as young adults.

How others react

Children pick up a lot from the behaviour of adults and others around them. Often it is unspoken and unexpressed, particularly anger, sadness and fear. They can learn very early in life that death is frightening and should not be talked about. As much as possible, have things out in the open. If you hide and keep things secret, the impression you give is that it is wrong to talk about them, that they are too big, bad or frightening.

DAD SAYS
DEATH ISN'T
SOMETHING
WE SHOULD
BE SHY OR
ASHAMED
TO TALK
ABOUT...

... SO IT'S
UNLIKE
HIS LINE
DANCING,
THEN.

Your children will take their cue from you. Particularly at this frightening time they will watch you closely. They will also watch other adults and older children for signs that will give them clues as to how they should behave and what is going on. Try to ensure that they are with family and friends who they trust and who will not be fearful, or who will not feed them superstitions or 'old wives' tales' about death and life hereafter.

INVOLVEMENT
I cannot over-stress the importance of keeping children involved at all stages. Too often children are excluded from this extremely important event in their lives, usually with the best of intentions. It is *not* helpful to exclude them and in most cases actually hinders their grieving and ability to recover.

The younger the child the more difficult it is for them to grasp the reality and permanence of death. It is difficult for us all. Anything that we can do to help children with this should be done. Seeing the deceased is probably the single most helpful thing for children. Unless the person has been badly maimed and looks really frightening, children can understand. Like a four-year-old friend of mine who went to see his dead grandmother and said, 'Oh, look at Granny – but it's not *really* Granny', and he ran off to play happily.

You may fear how children will remember the deceased. Like adults, they may remember them as dead for a while, but gradually the memory will fade and other memories, equally strong, will come back to give a balanced overall set of memories. Seeing the deceased may be another shock, but it is a shock that brings home the reality, which *must* be faced if they are to 'let go' of the deceased and move on with life eventually.

Helping Your Child Through Bereavement

CHAPTER 2: UNDERSTANDING DEATH

GETTING IT RIGHT

How to explain death to children of any age, when we cannot fully understand it ourselves, can be a daunting task. To encourage you, remember that *not* discussing it has more influence on children than almost anything 'wrong' you might say! Of course there is no 'wrong' way, perhaps just good and better. And you know best how to get through to your own children. Such a discussion is a *dialogue*, a two-way *process* that you can control as you go along.

WORKING OUT WHAT TO SAY TO MY KIDS ABOUT DEATH IS TOUGH...

OH, GIVE IT A GO — IT'S NOT GOING TO KILL YOU.

Remember that explaining about death is no more important than explaining about other issues and life events, such as birth, sex and generally how to be in the world. All of these are daunting but are, nonetheless, another part of parenting that you are swept along into whether you organise it or not! If you haven't discussed death with them before they experience it and you're thrown in at the deep end, you have no choice but to do your very best.

YOUR OWN BELIEFS

Every religion and culture and every family has its own way of regarding life and death, its own belief system. You will naturally want to pass yours on to your children.

This time of bereavement is one of the times you get the opportunity to do that in a direct way. So, tell your children what you want them to grow up thinking and believing in a way that you know they will understand. If they don't understand they will tell you.

LEVELS OF UNDERSTANDING

You know your own children much, much better than anyone else does. No one can judge better than you their level of sophistication in language, their emotional development, the effects of past experiences and their strengths and weaknesses. These are what determine their ability to understand death and to take in what has happened when someone close to them dies.

QUESTIONS

Sometimes you may get tired or even irritated with the number and repetitiveness of questions children ask. But value them; they are a most useful indication of what is going on for your children and what their needs are. Young children usually communicate simply and directly – sometimes embarrassingly so! Answer them equally simply and directly.

Take your cue from them and you will get the right language level for that particular child. Remember, each child is an individual, and sophistication of language does not always depend on age nor is it always a reflection of emotional sophistication or maturity.

Generally, children will ask all they want and need to know about the whole subject of death and bereavement. Unless, that is, they have picked up or sensed that the subject is taboo or is upsetting to those around them. In our society there is a lot of denial about death, resulting in it becoming a taboo subject. Older children especially can have picked up this taboo, if not in the home then in school and from peers, the media, etc.

ALWAYS ANSWER
- Always answer your children's questions;
- Always tell the truth, never lie;
- Never answer more than is asked – unless you sense strongly that they are really asking for more information than they are able to verbalise;
- Don't worry if they don't ask any questions – give them time.

Always answer, that is, always give *some* answer – even if it is to say you will tell them later (and be careful to do just that). Remember, the *way* you answer is as important as *what* you say. Children will sense denial, anger, embarrassment, etc. So answer as calmly and confidently as you can. If they repeatedly ask the same question it may be because:
- They are drawing attention to the fact that they are upset and need listening to, and need time to grieve in their own way;
- It is really a different question each time but they may not have the language skills to express it differently each time;
- They want to know more but for some reason won't or can't express that.

You know your own children so very, very well that you will be able to figure out which of the above is happening.

Tell the Truth. Tell *your* truth, insofar as you can of course. Never lie – lies or even euphemisms can land you in big trouble. If you give the impression that you have 'lost' granddad or that he has gone away to another country you will have an even more upset, fearful and confused child than if you tried to tell the truth in language he or she understands. If, and only if, the child uses metaphor, follow along with the same metaphor, for example;

Child: Will Claire be playing all day now that she is in heaven?
Parent: I expect so, I am sure she is very happy.

In this question the child is probably really asking if Claire is happy. She is using the metaphor for playing, which makes *her* happy.

Never answer more than the child asks, but leave space and time for more questions *just then* if possible – seize the moment. Never lecture children on the whole subject and its implications, they may not listen, or may be only able to take in what they have asked for.

No Questions? If the child doesn't ask questions it may be that he or she wants to avoid the bad feelings that bringing up the subject can evoke. Sometimes children are afraid of showing their vulnerability, and crying in front of other people may not be brave or cool. Again, given space and time and perhaps some encouragement, they will bring up the subject.

Very small children may only bring it up in play. Various rituals and anniversaries will give children opportunities to talk and ask questions.

CHAPTER 3: THE STAGES OF GRIEF OR HOW CHILDREN MIGHT FEEL

THE STAGES

When we learn that a loved one has died we just cannot let it all in at once. The pain of realisation would be too much to bear. Our basic survival instinct only allows us to let the bad news in little by little, i.e., in stages.

Nowadays, most people have at least heard of the 'stages of grief' and many would identify them as denial, anger, bargaining, depression and acceptance. These are some of the feelings we may experience after a death, or in fact after any trauma. There are many others – guilt, fear, anxiety, abandonment, fatigue, helplessness, despair and hope.

Children experience these too and, like adults, what and how they experience varies with each individual.

It is perfectly normal for children to feel any or indeed all of these feelings after a death. Which ones they will feel or will be with longer, or get 'stuck' at, will depend, like the whole grieving process, on the variables I have mentioned before, particularly their make-up and personality, who has died, the circumstances of death, their age, and previous life and death experiences.

THE FEELINGS

I will mention briefly a few guidelines as to how you might help your children to get through these feelings. They may only experience one or two, or they may go through the whole gamut. Children have faster reactions than we adults, so they may move quite quickly through these feelings and often appear to be moody or having mood swings. This is quite normal.

Denial/Disbelief/Numbness

- *Keep* children in touch with the reality of the death by bringing them to see the dead person and to the funeral.
- *Involve* them appropriately in all the other family gatherings and rituals.
- *Do not* try to *rub it in* by talking to them or at them.
- Involve them, when appropriate of course, but as much as possible in the *decisions and changes* that must be made in order to adjust to the absence of the deceased.
- If children talk or behave as if the deceased will be coming back, almost as if from a holiday, just *quietly remind them* that they will not be coming back, but do not labour it.
- Do not worry, *reality will dawn.*

Anger

Anger is the feeling most commonly expressed by grieving children, especially young ones. Anger can also be a sign of frustration, and the less verbal skills they have, the angrier they can be.

- *Allow* them to be angry – at you, and even at the deceased.

- Allow them to be quite irrational and unreasonable – do not argue it out with them or tell them they *should not* be angry and why.
- *Do not* point out that the *real* reason they are angry is because their father/mother/brother/sister, etc., has died.
- At a different time, when the anger is forgotten, you can have a conversation about how death can make us feel.

Bargaining

With children, a lot of bargaining happens in the realm of fantasy, or in their prayers, bargaining with God.

- If they share this with you, explain gently that nothing can bring a dead person back no matter what we do, or how good or well-behaved we are.
- Again, this bargaining is quite normal.

Depression

Yes, children do become depressed after a death but usually only deeply or 'clinically depressed' if they have not been able to grieve. If you think your child is seriously depressed, consult your family doctor or a professional counsellor. It is, however, quite normal for children to be extremely sad and to cry often and deeply.

- *Allow* them to cry, in fact encourage them. It can be difficult for them to allow this themselves, particularly boys, older children and teenagers.
- *Cry with them* if this comes naturally. It allows them to see that it is possible to cry and to recover and that it is not taboo in your family.
- *Respect* their need to be alone, to play sad music and to 'mope' around the house – even if it annoys or depresses you.

Guilt

Children up to the age of four or five often have a magical quality to their thinking and can imagine themselves as being powerful enough to cause a death by saying or even thinking that they wish a person were dead. This feeling can persist even into the teens. Many children carry this heavy burden for years. Vestiges of it can remain into adulthood, if in a rather vague way, or it can have been suppressed and remain buried.

- Always explain to your child as best you can the *real cause* of the death.
- If you suspect your child may be feeling this way, bring it up in conversation – explain that thoughts or things we say *cannot* cause someone to die.
- In the case of suicide do not suggest that the deceased was very sad or unhappy. Rather suggest that their thinking got very muddled and confused. Guilt is closely connected with responsibility. Make it plain that children are not responsible for how adults feel.

Fear

We are all afraid of death and of losing loved ones. Children, when confronted with death, fear both that they themselves and, more commonly, others close to them, will die.

- Allow them to *cling*. It is a phase and it will pass.
- Reassure them frequently, in whatever ways you can, of the health of others around them.
- Keep their environment as stable as possible.
- With older children, discuss in as matter-of-fact a way as possible what would happen if you or someone close should die, for example, who would care for them if left without parents. This is to reassure them that they won't be abandoned and to allay fears and fantasies about the future.

Anxiety

Anxiety is really a form of fear spread out, as it were, over all or many other issues. Everything for them may have taken on an uncertain or threatening feeling.

- Be patient, it will pass.
- Reassure constantly.
- Keep life as normal and as like it was before the death as possible.

Fatigue

Grieving is tiring for children too. They may not be sleeping or they may be having disturbed sleep and frightening dreams. Just before sleep is a time when a lot of fear and frightening fantasies surface.

- If you suspect this is happening, stay with them until they sleep.
- If appropriate, take them into bed with you, if they want, when they have nightmares or night terrors.
- Be lenient with days off school and pleas for lying on in bed.

Helplessness

Death engenders helplessness in us all, and in the face of such a momentous happening we are of course helpless. This is not a pleasant feeling.

- You can help to balance this by *contradicting* the feeling. Give children some tasks to do and some decisions to make. Keep an eye out to see that they succeed in whatever they do.
- Give them *responsibility* appropriate to their age and ability – and if necessary help them to carry it through to its conclusion.

Despair

Children can feel despairing – that there is no hope, no future and no way out. It tends to persist only in pre-adolescent and adolescent children.

- If your child is experiencing this depth of anguish for more than an occasional few hours, get professional help. Tragically, nowadays an increasing number of young people, young men in particular, are taking their own lives.
- With any teenagers, but especially with grieving ones, keep in communication. Keep talking *together*, do not talk at them. Maintain the *relationship*. Encourage them to express their depth of despair, no matter how it makes *you* feel. But, you do not have to carry this on your own, talk it over with a friend or family member whom you trust or with your doctor. Do your best to get your child to do the same.

Hope

'Hope springs eternal' and is a very natural way for us to instinctively contradict bad feelings surrounding death.

- If the child persists in hoping the deceased will return, let the reality dawn *slowly*. Do not contradict it too vehemently.
- Bring the conversation round at an appropriate time to other kinds of hope, for example, hope that the deceased won't be forgotten, that they are happy where they are, etc.

We are More Than Our Feelings

Perhaps sooner, perhaps later, those feelings will pass; they will certainly lose their intensity. Some will recur periodically even for a number of years. Explain this to your child, that feelings come and go – some days we feel good, other times we have a bad day. Explain that feelings are an important part of us but not all of what we are – we are body, feelings, mind and spirit.

CHAPTER 4: CAN I/SHOULD I PREPARE THEM?

IS DEATH A TABOO IN YOUR FAMILY?

Just as we prepare children in case they ever have to go to hospital, you can prepare them for the experience of a death. Don't treat death as a taboo subject in your family. When it is talked about, include the children. Hidden subjects and secrets engender fear. Things out in the open and talked about are not so huge and frightening. You will have some idea of how they are thinking and feeling about it.

FIRST EXPERIENCE OF DEATH

A child's first experience of death should never be, if at all possible, that of someone close to them. Take children, however young, to local wakes and funerals. Talk with them in a matter-of-fact way about death being a natural part of life, like flowers growing and maturing, getting old and dying. Explain that this usually happens when people are very old but can occasionally happen to younger people who have accidents or unusual illnesses.

In times when wakes were the norm, children ran in and out and usually went up and touched the corpse. They looked on the whole event with excitement, awe and a little fear too. It was really like some special, if unusual, kind of party. Now this kind of wake is less common, but they do take place, even in cities. If children haven't had the advantage of this kind of introduction to death, it's never too late to start. Be careful not to force them but encourage and include.

If they don't want to go to a wake or a funeral, or see a dead body for the first time, don't get into a power struggle. Encourage them to go with you or others in the family. Include them in rituals and arrangements, give them jobs or tasks to do. Ask them to be with younger children. Treat it as much as possible like any other family event.

Teenagers usually want to be with peers. So try to include some of their friends in whatever is happening or include yourself with them.

Children, like all of us, learn more from what they *sense* and perceive from the 'teacher' than from what is actually verbalised – hence the old adage 'do what mother says, not what she does'!

PLAY

One of the main ways children cope or deal with grief is through play; it is their therapy and you should encourage them. Usually they re-enact events that are troubling them (even if they are not aware of them or cannot articulate them). They may repeat these 'games' over and over again years after the event.

If they are not doing this and you feel they need help with their grief (remember you *cannot* take the pain away), try taking time to play with them. Allow them to choose the games. It is time-consuming and it may be hours, days, weeks or even months before they will play the 'healing' games. However, stay with it and try to be patient. It is important that *they* choose or suggest the games – *not* you. When they are ready the healing will take place.

In the game let them take the lead, direct the play, boss you and others around! This helps them to take some little power at a time in their lives when they may feel powerless or a victim of circumstances.

SHARING WITH OTHER CHILDREN

It is important for children to do some of their 'grief work' informally, away from adults, with peers whose outlook on life is similar to theirs. One of the ways they do this is in the kind of play discussed above. Another way is simply that they meet with other children of their own age and don't become isolated or spend too much time with adults. Sometimes it helps if you know families where children have had similar or somewhat similar experiences. Beware though; having suffered a bereavement is not enough reason for children to get along well together, or even to like each other!

There are some support groups for bereaved children, run by hospitals, schools, hospices, etc. If your children like the idea of these, you might suggest they go along. Like everything involved in helping them to grieve, *never* coerce or force them, no matter how much *you* would like them to go or how much it pains *you* to watch them suffering.

RITUAL AND REMEMBERING

I have mentioned the funeral and burial or cremation rituals previously. Very often, when recently bereaved adults, and children too, are shocked and numbed at the time of the death, a lot goes over their heads and they function in a dazed state – 'in automatic'.

Later it is often useful to attend and/or create other rituals that you and your children can be involved in together. Here are a few suggestions:

- Attend the Months Mind Mass, if this is part of your culture;
- Have a small gathering in the weeks following the death to thank family and close friends for their help at the time of the death. Take a little formal time to talk about the deceased;

- Do something formal on the deceased's birthday, like planting a special tree in the garden;
- Encourage children to write about or paint or draw the deceased. Maybe their school might put their piece in the school magazine or on the notice board – or you can put it up in your home;
- Suggest the child write a letter to the deceased and burn it in a little ceremony, maybe with some items of the deceased that need to be disposed of such as letters, etc.;
- On anniversaries – Christmas, birthdays, etc., – visit the grave or crematorium and bring flowers or plants.
- Put a special photo of the deceased in a prominent position in your sitting room or den and let the children keep fresh flowers in front of it.

All these rituals are ways of remembering the dead in a special and somewhat formal way. They mark the passing in a particular way in our minds and hearts. It is a very, very important way of *letting in* the fact that they have died and gone forever, thus enabling us to move on. It ensures that we are not forgetting them *even in moving on*, a fear so many carry. Never, never fear that in getting on with your life you will lose or forget your beloved. They are now, and always will be, a part of you in a way they could never be when alive, not necessarily a better way of course, but in a way that is itself very special.

CHAPTER 6: PROFESSIONAL HELP

GRIEF IS NOT AN ILLNESS

Grieving is not an illness; it is a perfectly natural process following a loss. It is our recovery mechanism. Without grieving in some way, it is extremely difficult, if not impossible, to recover. Children are fortunate in that their natural mechanisms are less damaged than ours and usually work better and faster. With permission from adults around them, and some encouragement from peers too in the case of older children, they will grieve and they will recover.

IS PROFESSIONAL HELP NECESSARY?

There are some situations in which it is more difficult for a child to grieve openly and easily. Some of these are when:
- parents are separated and one of them dies;
- both parents have died, either separately or at the same time;
- your child is in some way trying to be 'responsible', usually the eldest or an only child;
- when an adult is depending too much on the child;
- when their grief or loss is not acknowledged;
- when they are unable, for *any* reason, to express their feelings.

Some children do manage to grieve well in these circumstances, but it is unusual. If they are showing signs of grief after a long time has elapsed, or if their behaviour is interfering with their mental or physical health, their normal social life or the lives of those around them, look for professional help.

These signs can be:

- dropping behind badly in school work;
- bullying another child or acting violently;
- stealing, especially outside your home;
- refusing to go to school or to eat;
- spending an unusual amount of time alone or in their room or in bed;
- trouble with the law for any reason.

WHERE TO GO

If and when you have discussed the possibility of professional help with your child, whatever his or her age, the first step is to ask your family doctor, your child's teacher or an appropriate friend if they know a suitable counsellor, or consult the social services department of your local hospital.

If your child is under eighteen I would suggest that you consult the therapist yourself first. In this way you can decide if you think the therapist is suitable, explain the situation and discuss fees, etc. As I have said, some hospitals, hospices and other organisations run bereavement support groups for children. Your GP should know what is available in your area.

CHAPTER 7: CONCLUSION

To conclude, I would like to summarise a few of the most important ideas in this book:

- Each child is a *unique individual* and will grieve differently.
- *Remember* that you know your own children better than anyone else does.
- Take *good care of yourself* before, and while attending to your children.
- How children react is more about *who they are* than the circumstances of the death.
- Give children *time*, attention and encouragement to grieve.
- Talk openly about the deceased and the circumstances of his or her death.
- *Involve* children as much as possible in all the events surrounding the death, funeral, burial or cremation and other family rituals.
- *Do not hesitate* to get professional help if you are worried.
- Do your very best, you cannot do more.

CAN ADULTS LEARN TO HELP CHILDREN COPE WITH DEATH?

YES— AND YOU'RE LIVING PROOF!